T0114612

LOOK
LUSH

Sara Maya Webb

BALBOA.PRESS
A DIVISION OF HAY HOUSE

Balboa Press books may be ordered through booksellers or by contacting:

Balboa Press
A Division of Hay House
1663 Liberty Drive
Bloomington, IN 47403
www.balboapress.com
844-682-1282

Print information available on the last page.

ISBN: 979-8-7652-3195-1 (sc)
ISBN: 979-8-7652-3196-8 (e)

Balboa Press rev. date: 07/21/2022

Notes From the Author:

If you like what you see, please
leave a review for my book!

Reviews are incredibly helpful for authors.

Please consider reading these works in the
order they have been presented.

Dedication:

For Liliana, Grace, Julia, all womxn

Acknowledgements:

Warm appreciation to Susie Darin and Allison Nolen.

To Carla: I could not have written a word
without your love and support.

CONTENTS

PART I
LOOK

PART II
LUSH

PART

LOOK

Heal trauma through another's eyes
Digest this perception
Then take care to apply to the eyes on the inside
We all have the potential to heal, just by looking closely

Elixir

Sip these words
Roll them around on the tongue
of your mind

Allow each syllable
to slowly tumble down
to rumble

Bathe in these words
allow them to marinate
So the subconscious
can bubble
up

Make space
for the ideas to
nestle near
your soul

Transmute your creation
allow
your higher Self to
Heal

Seek

Looking is much more
than
seeing

Looking is much less
than
SEEKING

Seek truth, for freedom
can be found

~

At this
very moment
at any moment
at every moment

the one person
who can change
your life
infinitely
indefinitely
is
you

But first
do not
look
away

Data Processor

billions of bits of data
are always
around us

the human brain gobbles approximately
11 million bits
per second

but

we are aware of roughly
45 bits
of the 11 million

most of the data
our bodies ingest are
subconscious

we can only
consciously look at
.04%
of reality
each instant

here begin our gut feelings
and
feeling things in our bones
and
hair standing up
on backs of our necks

Reactions

instead of dissociation
or distraction

Look at the root
Anger
Sadness
Fear

Find the original trauma
but don't get stuck

flow ~ flow ~ flow
instead of
focus

Sometimes we laugh for minutes on
end until we cannot breathe
giggle until tears trickle

but
for big work
it may take
years of tears
until
we inhale
fully
and can belly laugh
again

Heal

Living with intention
demands
observation of our lives
from
above

It requires looking carefully
at the things
we
don't
want to
perpetuate

Consciously unpeeling
the layers
of perception
and
applying an upgraded
lens
to our chosen reality

First
we look
at the wound
however old it may be
hear its tales
by walking along its lines
until we are able to see
a scar
as utter beauty

Perception

Looks are ephemeral

and

only as we grow old
do we have
the unique opportunity
to choose to grow
more beautiful

I choose
to look for
and
appreciate
the Good
the Beauty
the Joy

Looking for Healing

The men who raped me
could have easily held me down
with
that
many
hands
but they used a drug
anyway

the physical wounds
have long ago
healed

Now looking at the rage
sitting in the sting
I feel a little heal
I see a seed
to grow

Silent Lion's Roar

I could not
have told
the man who held me at 8 minutes old
Looked, then said
he'd fight a lion for me

I thought I
could not have told the police
for
the perps had silenced my throat
used it for glee
rendering me powerless
leaving bruises for memories

I could not have told another soul, save my 23-year old
Sister
for the guilt I embodied
for the fear I'd be shunned
for the shame I'd be blamed

I speak about it now
not just to heal myself
not only to protect my daughters

but for the millions of womxn
still afraid to say
me too

Metamorphosis

They shushed my voicebox
along with my consciousness
several short hours
of my then-27-year old life

They tried to defile the box
between my legs
boxed
my face
propped me
outside a lobby
to wake at dawn

as I was last to learn of my fate
I squelched myself to silence
boxed my brain between
flimsy fences of foreboding humiliation

until I became
the
box

Oh, how that box served me.
Triage unit, initially
Chrysalis, finally

splutter-to-flutter

I raise my winged voice
so we can
all rise

Stardust

Looking within arouses

fear

Most people resist
petrified
of what they will find

but

quantum physics says we are unadulterated energy
sheer space
pure possibility

every cell
is
starlight

continue to peer
gaze deeper
within

pure potentiality
materializes

Midst of a Trigger

Look at the trauma
trite or tough

allow the
very next
look
to be the
emotions triggered
by
same similar events

Healing begins
when
whimper
becomes
waltz

Emotions

We can see something without intention
but to look
requires desire

magnifying glass
reveals that
FEAR
rules

Fear is the foe of Love – its precise opposite

Anger
is
fear
every iteration of it
resentment to rage
and all between

Sadness
is
fear – just look
at the ultimate
sadness:
grief

stripped down
is it not
fear
of coping
without
our dear loved
one

Guilt
plays variously
dressed up
assorted blends
of anger, fear, sadness

Look for love

find yourself

in love with your life

Words Have Weight

Change the way

you look at

obstacles

for

they are

springboards

Healing from the
Body Shock
has propelled me
to new limits
of
Strength

Meditation

We
have

5 senses

11 million sensory
receptors
in our bodies

10 million of them
are dedicated to
sight

When we close our eyes
we are better able to perceive
that which lies within

to look at that
which
the light
does
not
touch

Restoration

To heal body mind soul

get the gunk out
let it ooze
from your pores
yoga walk run yourself

Sit down
to practice
autonomic writing

pranayama through it

Breathe, intentionally, in provocative, methodical ways

Look to the ancients

Meditate
Meditate ~ Meditate
and meditate some more

Ask
out Loud
for divine assistance

Embody these practices

You don't need a grand plan

Just do
the
next right
thing

Magic

Manifesting is the most
beautiful form
of self-delusion

It is consciously choosing
to accept
only the reality
of our creation

Contemplation

Silence allows us to
look

Find time
Make time
Get quiet

Sit with eyes closed
Listen to the body

Patience

becomes

awareness

Carla

She
fills
spaces

inside
me

inside
my
broken
healing
heart

where
I never
knew
to
look

Take a Chance

Freedom

often

looks like

danger

Follow The Beam

Look for the
light

to see the
good

The light within
you

The light around
you

The light

that

is

you

Keys to Enlightenment

Look
for the
Good

Find
the
Joy

Fall
in
Love
with your own rich magnificence

E x p a n d
into
what you find

Your healing is inside
close your eyes
and
Look

PART

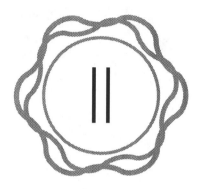

II

LUSH

lush /lʌʃ/ - from Oxford Online Learner's Dictionary

adjective:
- (vegetation) growing thickly and strongly in a way that is attractive

adjective:
- beautiful and making you feel pleasure

noun:
- a heavy drinker, especially a habitual one

Haikus

Diversions help not
musings persevere and slurp
delicious woman

lips slip-slide beneath
embracing her sweltering
embodiment of luscious

like meditation
she obfuscates regulation
cravings do not stop

alluring temptress
shadowy invitations
sip, gulp, guzzle, burp

Basking in her arms
glistening and pulsating
poetry trickles in

Closeting

In southern baptist suburbia
the cocktail infusion of geography and religion
condones drinking underage before spilling into
homosexuality

My parentages
did not drink at all
per pulpit protocols

They controlled contact
to the 'secular' hedonistic seething world
Limiting my exposure
to music movies dating dancing

Puberty
got me enrolled
in Passion for Purity
whose passion
was pushing abstinence

College a state away spelled
Freedom
few weeks in
sanctioned first forays
into the unwieldy world
of wine
which mixed well with women
until university days evaporated

young adulthood smacked
fellow females felt forbidden
I drowned my desire in shots, carafes, bottles,
until I couldn't even admit it to
myself

Dawdle

Sometimes when my lashes first flutter
dreamy musings
of her
dilly-dally
between my ears
behind my eyes
slip away to wishes
for her hips
  within
    reach
to sniff
  savor
    devour

Anticipation

Her essence remains
wisps of automatic thoughts
dissolve into her

Deceits, thievery
How did she steal orgasmic
capabilities

Inappropriate Noises

I miss
her hands
taunting me with word, image, vid
Simple grasps of leather steering
conjure grips on hips
knuckles decidedly strong
resisting flames, night, shade,
and distilling my raw edges

The scent of sun-speckled skin
Stretches of tawny perfection
over cachéd curves

seethe, lurch, snarl
Guttural depths of lungs
incite unbounded exploration
Gentle whimpers, outright yelps
her vocal folds whispering my name

Lost in lust, stuck and slipping between
her folds, undulations, delicate arches
blind by candlelight
palpating walls of
the
most
delicious desert ravine
on any plane yet tapped
mired in magic of mirage
fantasy of future
scenes, dreams
dissipate

Blues swallow me whole
eclipsing solitary stuffed olives
Secrets shaken, spilled upon
clawed vinyls
scribbled, crammed, suspended
Looming in odd lots
of empty bottles

Proximity

Her vicinity
invokes hips, lips, hands harken
womanly wills lurk

Cease tastiness
release me please, cannot be
addicted to you

Oblivious

even days the beach is
on mute,
the fierce loyalty
of Mother Nature
stands
stunning
in her authenticity

just a peek at dim morning light
She touches me effortlessly
waves seep
inside between around

tide to wave to grain
intentional and consistent

like wind against
puffballs of perspiration
slide below horizon
She remains
unyielding
in her hushed promise

Grateful Velocity

great Warren B warned of a single mouth
and two ears
So I try to
sit quietly when in doubt
release control every goddess
lest bacchus boomerang

Love notes pierce syringe-like
rearview images resurface
linger
like pupils across
knuckles and fingers

The afternoon splashed
orchestral
triggers of plural murals
slingshot me
armorless to her
Tiered lairs fog my focus wheel
dust from a stump grinder

Our paragraph of growth
sent me subterranean
to the original soul inside
where no finger can fondle
Perspective of sanity's feedback
spark of emotions
dammed up
release apologies to my outer child

Growth can also be cancerous
swift centrifuge
merry-go-round
replacing merrily forward
on the Happy Road of destiny

Simple daily starts
of consistent
Gratitude
and the shift is seismic

Alchemy

We began at the branches,
transitioned to trunk and twig

I can still hear the rustle of palms
the lightness - a freedom
of existence
of being without boundaries

Fronds sway in windy flux
carrying humid aromatic whispers of perspective
and surrender

Sipping her sweet elixir into me
smooth
syncopation

The entice of each story sprinkles droplets of thoughts
which simultaneously speckle
drop
between us like the pulse
beat of electric air
yet
mid air
cell to cell, in organic motion,
conversations
without words
across the expanse
of inexplicable connection

Summer nights repeat anew
conjuring crisp memories
sweat, sun and slumber
Swallowing her scent
as we coalesce

She Demanded Poetry

The one woman, tolerated despite desired
solitude
beyond punctuated celibacy

Why do I
perceive her innocent

Why do I
crave her caresses
across the sterile miles

Why do I
abide her weighty wishes

Communication or delusion
inherent mis-understandings
of intentionality
nevertheless
there remain three sides to every story

Ex-non-girlfriend

You wondered
what we talked about
that night

you talked
I listened
and mostly stiffened
especially
when we embraced

I was honest
and also
firm

there were so many tears
especially
after you left

Self-Discovery

I was taught to
bottle up
emotions
tendencies
proclivities
any differentiation that might upset another

I learned how to unleash them
on crucial battlefields

I was nimble
bottling up my truth
each one flasked individually

Some nights they would clang together
enough corks popped, they'd foam over me
in lieu of rational discussion over coffee served with sanity

Spontaneous Combustion

When creativity's shadow descends
follow her allure, however terrifying

Swallow her fleeting gift whole
and begin your brew

Embark on the journeys she inspires

Dreams materialize like symphonies
yet begin with firefly whispers

First tendrils of night knead my eyeballs
suspended in the twitching air
becoming one with the fireflies

Pure Intentionality

Rumination
impressions of a summer ago

addict inside feeds, fuselol
for devious interludes

however constant, flavor and container shifts
desire
scampering through synapses

Muse fleets in retreat
absence nevertheless generates
negative space
seduced
again
by her deft dance
Chameleon colored stories slink amid
grey brain folds

shame dressed up like Love
fedora of deceit
loafers of regret

Intoxicate
fester
fixate
jerk to final fumble

frolic within the
expanding
open edged frame of
autonomous
self-determination

Temperance

Monotonous moment to moment
To the next dull, alcohol-less
moment
Each longer
unbroken instances link to next breath
Stark surprise of reality's gentle swing
bracing
for the next wave of emotion
Unable to explain the moments to anyone
and worse yet - unable to drink over it

Corona

I used to call myself a lush
laughing at the admission
while getting lushed up

Sobriety set in
before quarantine was called

Without wine
days
drone
hover
propelled along
by-the-second disease alert tracks
seclusion screams
corpses accumulate
spider webs in retail corners

Fear peppers us in our homes
most streets bleak
each day disintegrates
blowing into the next

60 Days and 1,000 Nights

Curvaliscious
bottle contents
heavy yet formless
inhabiting
its own space
then space between thoughts
and eventually
our spaces
if only by trace evidence

After I extinguished the fire of
dulling my own consciousness
its pull is palpable

In its absence
radical
inexplicable
emotional tension

We cling to It, in the spaces between obligations,
creating spaces
in our memories
at which we guess
or cringe

Friendly Friend

Dilated pupils
gulp
luscious lips
teeth, lungs

in excruciatingly sober moments
her words gush
over impassioned tongue

knighting me
Stunning Alluring Brilliant
her Dream Girl

My own conception then
so jaded and bent
that I never stopped to ask myself
if she
was mine

Immersion

Seagulls dare not dip nor taunt
cacophony of beats
vibrate
lively polka dots of people
along the
edge
of the earth

Sunscreen sticky scent
miles and hours removed
from the pulse of the beach waves
yet I am with her
bathing
in
her
energy
sprays of sand and salt
scorch me
anew

Lilt of her laughter still
makes my insides twirl in utter delight
twenty toes wiggle and slice
trillions of grains
of manifest
joy

Volcanic evidence in all her splendor
From destruction comes beauty
if given time to
simmer
   sort
     settle
       and groove

Anticipation of Actual Grandeur

As goddesses celebrate release from
addiction's talons
perhaps I will eventually shed tears
of joy
Marinating this moment
the only texture is gratitude

Fermentation

Pursuits of success, pursuits of the flesh
lubricate easily
with application of runny spirits
Shopping with abandon
is fueled and fanned with liquid grapes

Each quest only mired me further
into someone's prefabricated ideal
wedged into corners of fancy brown paper bags
perforating my existence
memory
and personality

Freedom from provocative proclivities
has me free
wide open
with an appetite for peace
and the full barrel of life

Painting with Words

Syllables like piano staccatos
gambol about synaptic associations
She used to
drown
out
the others

Muse of dreams dissipates to reveal
snares tightly woven
ephemeral wisps of hope

Luscious balance of focus and relax

6 Months of Sobriety

The pleasure
of being present

Giggle Lick
is the yogurt
off the top foil

Sunday at The Beach

Gull calls punctuate memories
of quick hearts with no plans
except giggles and ice cream
Rules loose made on the fly
Like only carefree girls can

Long-Lost Bestie

I almost walked
right past
the blue upstairs door
of destiny

timid knock

She smiled
and said
what are you doing here

I said - I came to find you

The best hug ensued

Soulmate

I see her often
in waking dreams
Her presence is palpable
No matter the distance

She's exquisitely robed in
Strength and Honesty

Her melody's promises waft,
gentle and powerful as
the invigorating breeze
of a peak's well-earned vista

Nooks

Memories snap fresh
my lips' corners creep
sly ponder of release
creases
curves
glint of a gaze
we intersect
dance as one
locked yet unbounded

Halloween

Daily discoveries knead my heart
above butterflies in bellies

Tittering slivers
surreptitious gazes
caught, never held

no tricks
only astounding treats
of her craft

Fingertips salivate
capillaries and
incantations rumble, assemble

Futile avoidance of submission
groan befalls moan

Her name remains
newly minted limerick on my lips
she is somehow
familiar and eloquent

Wide-eyed earlobes drool
longing for the touch of
her lips' whisper

Where women have been lost
in the ocean blue of
her eyes

I feel found
and
finally seen

Power

sweat simmers
slides
bodies like instinct
curves compel capillaries to ignition
fingertips stroke Lips
lids flutter to
submission

Answers within The Riddle

Poetry runs over my tongue
Liquid words spill
Down her neck

Syllables assemble their stance
and tickle
my slender mind like tender fingertips
Pulling me into her webb of deception

Passion
penetrates and
echos reverberate
roll about
then fall in line
obedient children
pleas drawn in silence across the expanse
innate knowledge
Twisted only by perception

Groping about the black night
of karmic debt
Freshly grown fear floats upon the stagnant swamps
Ripe for the bold of souls
the puzzles of one's own accord
with reality
The answer is the obstacle

For Carla

Her words
at once profound and tender
melt
around
my heart

I stagger, sober yet
clumsily humbly
in awe
As she nimbly enumerates
with eloquence of a goddess
my deepest desires
for pursuit of partnership

Divine timing she said
Stunned
I resound
yes

Her commitment and ambition
finally matches for my own
Evidence our ardent work
with others and in solitude

Independent as we are,
where do I stop and she begin

The two points of light
now seem one

We arrive fully formed for the other
in this. very. moment
this lifetime

For the angels spin songs of
countless lifetimes before
Melodies tuning time
for a new understanding of
the infinite universe

Vast expanse of the bay between
reminds me
sweetly
of the salty skin water

Too many midnights
already
Without her touch
longing for her fingertips' reach
and sweet caresses
between her sheets
Nestled between her thighs
and safe in her embrace
sweat
slips across glistening curves
like the gentle slide of
heartfelt tears of joy
I have shed in awe of her most welcome return to me

Yet a few too many nights remain
to lock lips and
harmonize our hearts once again

Nevertheless we are connected
across the mélange of Mother Nature
and mixed concrete

For we control time, we
patient and persistent warrior women
who have both
laid down our last weapon

Upon Waking

Her words quench my soul
gently swirl
among the listening lobes
of my heart

As I pull on the tee that
last lay on me between her sheets
it still carries whispering reminders
of rest and caress
my tongue can almost taste her
ever-present-essence
like spritely fairies frolicking
the rooms of my mind
she loiters
sweetly sticky like the scent
of an unexpected embrace from a robust woman's delicate
perfume

Powerfully expansive yet
humble and
visibly committed to embracing her full magnificence that I
cannot help but
bask in

She is the poem daily on my lips
the handsomest manifestation I could possibly conjure

Paradigm Shift

Previously
to me
Divine Love
only
could be
unconditional

but
it is a resolution
beginning inside
oneself

The fierce
simple
choice
to stand
open-eyed
broad-chested
fully facing fragile fear
repelling low vibrations
revealing majestic love

Window

Blinded by
fear
anger
hatred
projection

Resentment gremlins
trap us
inside our own selves
obscuring
the softest
the strongest

When we fully invite
Forgiveness into our bodies
to stay
it brings awareness along
in all its
many pockets

It may require
years
of
tears
bucketfulls
of breathwork
until our eyes can inhale
long enough
to see ourselves fully formed
Forgiveness washes the windows of the soul
entirely
greedy gremlins gone

Humility extends lashes
to catch the flies of discomfort
in perpetuity
compassion sparkles upon the surface

Once we can see
through forgiveness
we cannot go back to
tainted perceptions
of hatred and self-pity

Taking happiness in
Allowing rampant joy
requires powerful resistance
to the ease of negativity

Fortress
to
free fall forgiveness

Printed in the United States
by Baker & Taylor Publisher Services